AIKIDO, like all other martial arts, Asian and European, derives from fighting skills originally developed and used for hand-to-hand combat. It has evolved into one of the most beautiful of the formal, stylized representations of the ancient *jitsu*, now practiced primarily for recreation, fitness, and self-expression through movement.

THREE STYLES of aikido are presented -- an early style, a classical style, and a modern version using characteristic aikido actions and gestures.

BOKATA solo routines are represented by three examples of *kata* performed with the aikido long staff.

BOOKS BY BRUCE TEGNER

BRUCE TEGNER'S COMPLETE BOOK of SELF-DEFENSE

BRUCE TEGNER'S COMPLETE BOOK of JUJITSU

SELF-DEFENSE: A BASIC COURSE

SELF-DEFENSE NERVE CENTERS & PRESSURE POINTS

KARATE & JUDO EXERCISES

STICK-FIGHTING: SPORT FORMS

STICK-FIGHTING: SELF-DEFENSE

SAVATE: French Foot & Fist Fighting

JUDO: Sport Techniques for Physical Fitness & Tournament

DEFENSE TACTICS for LAW ENFORCEMENT:
     Weaponless Defense & Control and Baton Techniques

KUNG FU & TAI CHI: Chinese Karate & Classical Exercise

KARATE: BEGINNER TO BLACK BELT

JUDO: BEGINNER TO BLACK BELT

BOOKS BY BRUCE TEGNER & ALICE McGRATH

SELF-DEFENSE & ASSAULT PREVENTION FOR GIRLS & WOMEN

SELF-DEFENSE FOR YOUR CHILD

SOLO FORMS OF KARATE, TAI CHI, AIKIDO & KUNG FU

Also available from Thor Publishing Company

ELLEN KEI HUA BOOKS

KUNG FU MEDITATIONS & Chinese Classical Wisdom

WISDOM from the EAST

MEDITATIONS of the MASTERS

AIKIDO & BOKATA
by BRUCE TEGNER

THOR PUBLISHING COMPANY   VENTURA   CA   93002

Library of Congress Cataloging in Publication Data

Tegner, Bruce.
  Aikido & bokata.

  Includes index.
  1. Aikido. I. Title. II. Title: Aikido and bokata.
GV1114.35.T433   1983   796.8'154   83-4871
ISBN 0-87407-039-2 (pbk.)

AIKIDO & BOKATA

First edition: October 1983

AIKIDO & BOKATA

Copyright © 1983 by Bruce Tegner &
                            Alice McGrath

THOR PUBLISHING COMPANY   POST OFFICE BOX 1782

VENTURA   CA   93002

BRUCE TEGNER BOOKS REVIEWED

KARATE: BEGINNER to BLACK BELT
"Techniques and routines...illustrated in profuse detail...
specially geared to a Y.A. audience."
                                    KLIATT YOUNG ADULT PB GUIDE

SELF-DEFENSE: A BASIC COURSE
"An eminently practical, concise guide to self-defense...for
young men..."   American Library Association BOOKLIST

"YA - A calm, nonsexist approach to simple yet effective self-
defense techniques...clear photographs...sound advice."
                                    SCHOOL LIBRARY JOURNAL

BRUCE TEGNER'S COMPLETE BOOK OF JUJITSU
"...authoritative and easy-to-follow text..."
                                    SCHOOL LIBRARY JOURNAL

BRUCE TEGNER'S COMPLETE BOOK OF SELF-DEFENSE
Recommended for Y.A. in the American Library Association
                                    BOOKLIST

SELF-DEFENSE & ASSAULT PREVENTION FOR GIRLS & WOMEN (with
Alice McGrath)
"...should be required reading for all girls and women..."
                                    WILSON LIBRARY BULLETIN

"...simple and straightforward with no condescension...easy to
learn and viable as defense tactics..."   SCHOOL LIBRARY JOURNAL

SELF-DEFENSE FOR YOUR CHILD (with Alice McGrath)
[For elementary school-age boys & girls]
"...informative, readable book for family use..."
                                    CHRISTIAN HOME & SCHOOL

DEFENSE TACTICS FOR LAW ENFORCEMENT
"...an excellent textbook for a basic course in self-defense..."
                                    LAW BOOKS IN REVIEW

"...a practical tool for police academy programs, police programs
at the university level, and for the (individual) officer..."
                                    THE POLICE CHIEF

SELF-DEFENSE NERVE CENTERS & PRESSURE POINTS
"...a practical guide to the most effective weaponless self-defense
using the least possible force..."   THE POLICE CHIEF

KUNG FU & TAI CHI: Chinese Karate and Classical Exercise
"...recommended for physical fitness collections."
                                    LIBRARY JOURNAL

SOLO FORMS of Karate, Tai Chi, Aikido & Kung Fu (with Alice McGrath)
"...well-coordinated, step-by-step instructions...carefully captioned
photos...for personal enjoyment and exercise..." YA
                                    American Library Association BOOKLIST

CONTENTS

INTRODUCTION

Aikido is one of the most beautiful of the stylized weaponless fighting arts. It is good exercise, esthetically pleasing
to perform and observe, and it is intriguingly exotic.
Aikido can be as active as tumbling and as subtle and
refined as fencing. It can be practiced for recreation,
physical agility and self-expression through movement.

Like all martial arts, Asian and European aikido derives
from skills originally used in hand-to-hand combat.

The techniques of aikido have been known for thousands
of years. The characteristic style of present-day aikido was
developed relatively recently. The precursor of aikido was
aiki jitsu. It consisted of techniques of bending, twisting,
and applying pressure against the finger, wrist, elbow and
shoulder joints. Pain, immobilization, even fractured carti-
lage can result from the application of such holds and locks,
especially if they are applied with force.

The difference between aiki jitsu and aikido is not in the
techniques, but in the style of gesture and movement and
in the method of learning and practicing them.

Morihei Uyeshiba, a Japanese master of many types of
jujitsu, originated the mode of what we now recognize as
aikido. Instead of competing against an opponent in order
to develop proficiency, students in the Uyeshiba school
were taught to cooperate with a partner to learn the techniques. The rolling-out falls and the going-with mode were
introduced to allow partners to coordinate their actions.

Uyeshiba incorporated the formal manner of attack/defense
sequences common in many styles of jujitsu. Most aikido
practice involves learning the pre-arranged series of attack/
defense moves *(kata)* and performing them with many repe-
titions to develop technical skill and graceful movement.

HOW AIKIDO IS PRACTICED

Students learning and practicing aikido are not expected to endure pain or to risk injury. The three major safety procedures are: coordinated movements, rolling falls, and a release/submission signal.

GOING WITH

Aikido kata routines are performed without resistance. Partners follow a mode of *going with;* each one moving with the action.

Uke (oo keh) is the partner who simulates the attack and then is controlled by *nage* (nah geh). Uke and nage respond to each other. When nage performs the defense and control techniques, uke offers no resistance. Nage moves with uke's body movement to help ease uke to the mat, to allow uke to take a safe fall, and to prevent injury.

1,2. For example, as nage, shown left, applies a wrist twist and pushes uke backward, uke goes with the action by taking a back rolling fall.

3,4. A similar technique used against someone not trained in aikido would probably result in a response such as shown in photo 4. The response in photo 2 is not automatic and does not follow from the action naturally.

5,6. It can be seen that the response to the wrist/twist "throw" in photo 5 is a trained response. The action in photo 6 does not naturally follow from the action in photo 5. A more likely result would be pain or injury to the wrist.

AIKIDO FALLS

Learning the rolling safety falls is a prerequisite to practice and performance of the aikido katas. There is considerable risk of pain and/or injury if students attempt to learn the routines before achieving skill in the rolling falls.

Aikido falls resemble falls used in wrestling and in sport judo, but they are softer. In wrestling and judo the players may be thrown straight down with force and they must know how to absorb body impact as they hit the mat. In Aikido, uke rolls with the action to prevent pain and/or injury to the joints.

1

2

3

4

5

6

TAPPING FOR SAFETY

Tapping is the "release" or "stop" signal which is used at the conclusion of each segment of a kata if the ending is a control hold. Tapping may be used at any other time during practice or performance of a kata if nage is being rough or inadvertently applying a technique in a manner which causes pain, or if uke believes that it is appropriate to stop the action to prevent pain or injury.

Two light taps onto the mat, onto the partner, or at the body where pressure is being applied, are the ways in which the "stop" signal is made. Upon the tapping signal, there must be immediate release or stopping of the action.

Colored belts are awarded for proficiency. The novice wears a white belt, but there is no standard for colors to indicate advancement. Requirements for promotion to higher ranks vary from area to area and from instructor to instructor.

The hall or gym where aikido is practiced is called a *dojo*. The *hakama* aikido uniform (worn by Dr. Lodi and Mr. Wallace, page 78) is usually reserved for degree holders and in some instances, at the discretion of the instructor, is worn exclusively by those who have achieved black belt proficiency.

Although Uyeshiba introduced aikido in this century, there are already distinct styles and sub-styles throughout the world where it is practiced. The earliest variations were made by teachers who had been students of Uyeshiba.

AIKIDO FOR SELF-DEFENSE?

In my view, aikido has little relevance to modern self-defense. My opinion that aikido is not practical is based on my definition of what is modern, practical and appropriate *for most people:*

> Self-defense should consist of a relatively small group of techniques which most people can learn in a fairly short time.

> It should be available as a functional skill without constant practice.

> It should be available to people who are not in peak physical condition.

> Self-defense should include responses appropriate to the threat--from mildly threatening to life-threatening.

Aikido does not meet any of the criteria listed above. Of course, an expert in aikido, or an expert in any form of fighting, could use it for self-defense. Most people do not have the time or inclination to become expert.

The most enthusiastic advocates of aikido for self-defense acknowledge that it takes years to achieve functional skill. That fact alone would eliminate aikido as a practical option for many.

The skill to perform aikido techniques quickly and correctly is achieved through diligent practice. Skill diminishes unless practice continues. Most people do not have time or inclination to devote themselves to years of ongoing practice.

Because the principal mode of aikido practice is in formal routines which are prearranged and unchanging, there is a tendency to think in terms of specific attack/defense actions. This is appropriate in aikido practice but it does not correspond to life situations.

In the routines you will note that, regardless of the degree of seriousness of the "attack", the responses are always as if to "worst case" situations. To respond to hair-pulling or shoulder grabbing in the same manner as to a choke assault is, in my opinion, neither practical nor appropriate.

A response that is more violent than the intended insult does not meet the ethical standard of self-defense--using the least possible force to cope with the actual situation.

In the performance of the routines, the partners do not hurt each other so the question of force does not apply. But, if the same techniques were used on the street upon a person not trained in rolling gracefully out of the hold, there would be considerable pain and/or risk of dislocation or fracture. To risk such injury in defense against a serious assault could be justified; to risk such injury in a less threatening situation could not.

Almost all aikido defenses include a control-hold ending with the "assailant" on the ground. Law enforcement officers and medical and psychiatric personnel are sometimes required to restrain and immobilize a subject. The lay citizen does not have that responsibility and in most instances personal safety is ensured through avoidance and escape or by the use of a simple defense action which does not include trying to control/immobilize the person threatening or attempting assault.*

Aikido includes many techniques which are not easy to learn. Those who have difficulty learning body-movement skills can enhance eye-hand coordination through the practice of aikido, but it is unlikely that they could apply aikido for functional use.

Then what of the pictures and demonstrations of frail, old gentlemen easily disposing of multiple assailants with the light twist of the wrist? The frail old gentleman has been practicing aikido for most of his life. He is probably the master teacher "disposing" of students who have been trained to respond to the twist of the wrist. It would be grossly impertinent and discourteous for the strong young men to avoid, resist, or attempt a counter-twist upon the master.

* Ed. note: Tegner and Tegner/McGrath self-defense books are available from Thor Publishing Company, Ventura, CA 93002.

7

Finally, aikido routines still include attack/defense situations which do not apply. Defenses from the kneeling position, as in photo 7, are still included in some aikido courses.

SPIRIT

Uyeshiba's system was based on a quasi-religious, mystical concept of a "universal cosmic power" called *ki*. Concentration and a "sincere belief in its existence" would, he thought, produce a flowing out of ki and result in physical, moral and spiritual benefits. Superhuman strength and capabilities were ascribed to ki; the loss of ki was said to be the cause of illness and death.

My own world/life view is such that I do not accept the claim that aikido or any other martial art brings spiritual uplift. Exactly the same claims for moral, ethical, spiritual and worldly benefits were made for judo before it became an Olympic Games event.

In the thirty years during which I have been involved in this field -- teaching, researching, and writing -- I have not observed evidence to support such claims. I have not seen evidence that practitioners of the martial arts lead their lives on a higher spiritual, moral or ethical level than do other people. For you young people who are the major interest group , I propose that you play the martial arts for fun, fitness and health. For spiritual improvement, try compassion and kindness to your fellow humans.

— *ALICE McGRATH*

FIRST KATA - SUSAN HAINES & BRUCE CAMPBELL

This is a characteristic aikido kata.

Susan and Bruce rehearsed and practiced the routine to achieve coordinated, flowing movements and graceful gestures. Bruce simulates the attacks and does not resist the defense actions. Susan applies very light pressure; Bruce falls to the mat by going with her movements. Because their movements are coordinated, Bruce goes down without danger of being hurt. At the conclusion of each segment Susan simulates the application of the ending control hold.

†In unison, Susan and Bruce approach the practice area.

8. In unison they bow with their heads lowered. This is a symbolic gesture to indicate courtesy to the *dojo* (practice hall or gym).

9. In unison they bow to the *sensei* (instructor).

10. They step around to face each other and bow.

†
Throughout the text the numbered paragraphs are keyed to the photos which correspond.
When there is *no photo* to illustrate a move, the symbol † is used.

8   9

10

11

12

13

14

WRIST GRIP

11. Bruce grips Susan's right wrist with his left hand.

12. Susan twists her captured wrist and places her left hand at Bruce's wrist . . .

13. . . . and releases her right wrist as she grips his left wrist.

14. She grips his hand with both hands, placing her fingers into his palm and her thumbs at the back of his hand.

15

16

17

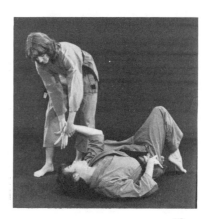
18

15. Susan twists his captured hand and wrist back and outward and . . .

16. . . . starts to turn clockwise as she continues the twisting action . . .

17. . . . which Bruce responds to by going with her movement as she continues to turn clockwise, wheeling Bruce around until . . .

18. . . . she has made a 3/4 turn and Bruce is on the mat on his back. Susan has maintained the grip on Bruce's hand throughout the turn; she leans forward as he goes down.

19

19. She drops onto her right knee and simulates additional pressure on the captured hand and wrist.

†Bruce taps the mat to indicate submission to the hold. They rise and face each other, ready for the next segment of the kata.

20   21

CROSS-BODY WRIST GRIP

20. Bruce grips Susan's right wrist with his right hand.

21. Susan twists her captured wrist out, down and around and . . .

22

23

24

25

22. . . . grips Bruce's right wrist with her right hand.

23. As Susan starts to wheel Bruce around clockwise, she pulls his captured arm across her body and places her left forearm at his elbow, maintaining the grip as . . .

24. . . . she continues the wheeling action . . .

25. . . . until he goes onto the mat . . .

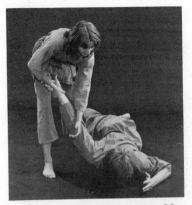

26

27

26. . . . face down and . . .

27. . . . Susan drops to her left knee and simulates the pressure of pushing down with her left arm as she pulls up on the captured wrist.

†Bruce taps to indicate submission. They rise, ready for the next segment of the kata.

28

29

30

31

TWO-HAND GRIP OF ONE WRIST

28. Bruce grips Susan's right wrist with both hands.

29. Susan twists her captured wrist and hand around to . . .

30. . . . grip Bruce's right wrist.

31. As she turns clockwise, she places her left forearm at his elbow and . . .

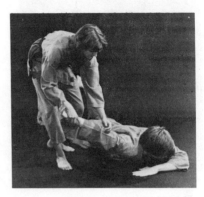

32   33

34

32. . . . continues the wheeling action which Bruce follows
by . . .

33. . . . going onto the mat, face down.

34. Susan drops to her left knee and simulates pushing down
on his elbow as she pulls up on his captured wrist with light
pressure.

†Bruce taps. They rise, ready for the next segment of the
kata.

35

36

37

38

DOUBLE WRIST GRIP

35. Bruce grips Susan's wrists.

36. She effects release by pushing outward with both arms, then . . .

37, 38. . . . she twists free by bringing her hands in, and up.

39   40

41

†She grips his right wrist with her right hand and . . .

39. . . . wheels him around and . . .

40. . . . down . . .

41. . . . and drops onto her left knee for the ending. Bruce taps.

†They rise, ready for the next segment of the kata.

42

43

44

45

CLOTH GRIP

42. Bruce grips cloth with his right hand, as shown.

43. Susan raises her left arm and . . .

44. . . . brings it over and . . .

45. . . . around Bruce's arm, then . . .

46

47

48

46. . . . raises her left hand to . . .

47. . . . place her left forearm across his right forearm as she starts to turn clockwise, then . . .

48. . . . as she continues to turn, she places her right forearm across his elbow.

49

50

51

49. She maintains the hold as she wheels him around . . .

50. . . . down . . .

51. . . . onto the mat, face down. She applies light pressure, pulling into her body with both arms. Bruce taps.

†They rise, ready for the next segment of the kata.

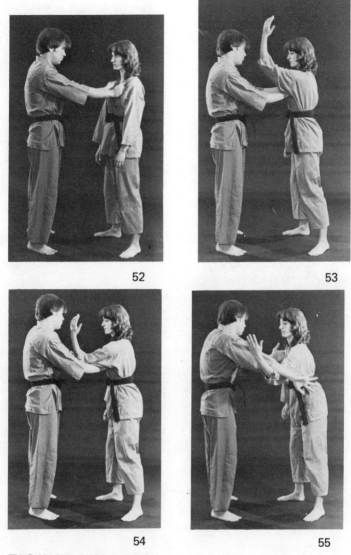

52

53

54

55

TWO-HAND CLOTH GRIP

52. Bruce grips cloth with both hands.

53. Susan raises her left arm and . . .

54. . . . drops her elbow over Bruce's right arm then . . .

55. . . . drops her left hand and brings it outside of his arm
to release his grip.

56

57

58

59

56. As she begins to turn clockwise, she capture's Bruce's right arm with her bent left arm and . . .

57. . . . clamps it into her chest as she wheels him around and . . .

58. . . . down as she clamps her right arm against his captured arm and . . .

59. . . . takes him to the mat, face down. She drops onto her left knee and applies light pressure. Bruce taps.

†They rise, ready for the next segment of the kata.

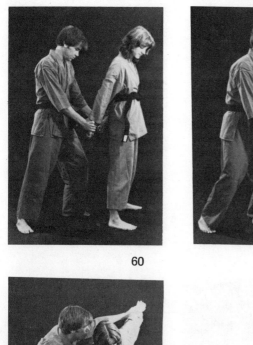

60

61

62

DOUBLE WRIST GRIP FROM THE BACK

60. Bruce grips Susan's wrists.

61. Susan presses outward slightly with both arms and, as Bruce simulates the reaction of pushing inward to counteract her movement . . .

62. . . . she steps and turns clockwise as she flings her left arm back and up and continues to turn . . .

63

64

65

63, 64. . . . until she is facing him.

65. She thrusts her left arm outward to effect release as she twists her right hand around and over to grip his right wrist.

66

67

68

69

66, 67. She pulls his captured arm cross-body as she starts another clockwise turn and places her left forearm at the back of his elbow . . .

68. . . . wheeling him around and down . . .

69. . . . onto the mat. She simulates the ending by pulling up on his captured wrist as she presses lightly with her forearm. He taps.

†They rise, ready for the next segment of the kata.

70   71

72   73

DOUBLE ARM GRIP FROM THE BACK

70. Bruce grips cloth at Susan's elbows.

71. Susan starts to turn clockwise as . . .

72. . . . she thrusts her left arm outward and . . .

73. . . . continues to turn . . .

74

75

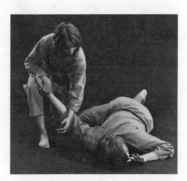

76

74. . . . to face Bruce. She grips his right wrist with her
right hand as . . .

75. . . . she frees her left arm and places it onto his captured arm, pulling his arm with her right hand. She continues
to turn, . . .

76. . . . wheeling him around and down onto the mat. She
applies light pressure. He taps.

†They rise, ready for the next segment of the kata.

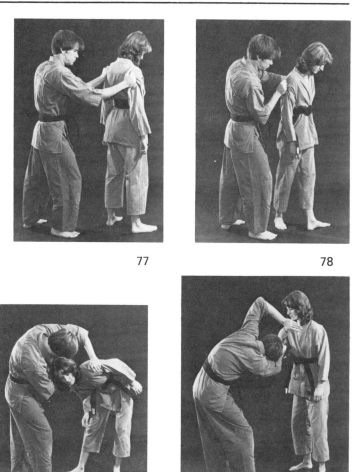

77

78

79

80

SHOULDER GRIP FROM THE BACK

77. Bruce grips cloth high on Susan's arms.

78. Susan starts to turn clockwise and . . .

79. . . . ducks down and . . .

80. . . . comes up, rising between his arms to release his left hand grip. She grips his right wrist with her right hand.

81

82

83

81, 82. As she pulls his captured arm, she places her left forearm at his elbow and turns clockwise . . .

83. . . . wheeling him around and down onto the mat. She applies light pressure. He taps.

†They rise, ready for the next segment of the kata.

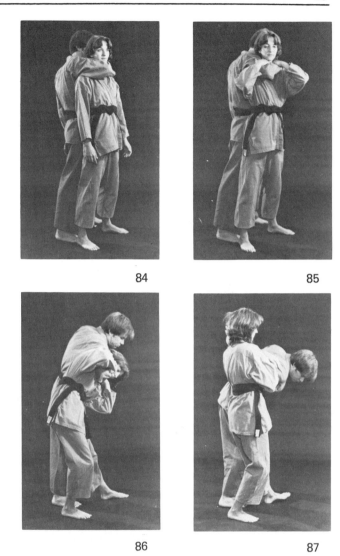

84

85

86

87

ONE-ARM CHOKE

84. Bruce places his right arm around Susan's neck, simulating a choke with very light pressure.

85. She grips his arm with both hands.

86. Pulling down on his arm . . .

87. . . . she backs out of his grip as she captures his arm and pulls it back and up.

88   89

88, 89. She applies the hold and drops onto her left knee to take him to the mat.

†He taps. They rise, ready for the next segment of the kata.

90   91

OVER-ARMS BODY GRAB

90. Bruce holds Susan with his arms over her arms.

91. Susan steps back with her right foot and . . .

92

93

94

95

92. . . . ducks down under his arm and . . .

93. . . . places her left arm over his right elbow and . . .

94. . . . as she takes another step back with her left foot she applies the hold.

95. She drops onto her left knee to take him to the mat.

†He taps. They rise, ready for the next segment of the kata.

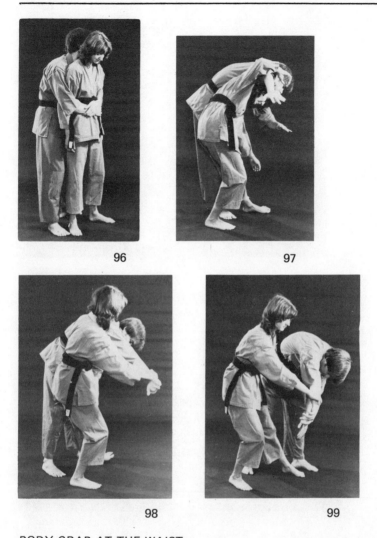

96   97

98   99

BODY GRAB AT THE WAIST

96. Bruce grabs Susan with both arms over her arms.

97. As she steps back, she thrusts both her arms up and . . .

98. . . . grips his right wrist with her right hand.

99, 100. As she pulls his captured arm back, she takes a step back with her left foot.

100 101

101. She pulls up on his captured arm and drops to her left knee to take him to the mat. She applies light pressure with her left forearm at the back of his elbow.

†He taps. They rise, ready for the next segment of the kata.

102 103

STRAIGHT PUNCH

102, 103. As Bruce simulates a straight punch, Susan parries his arm, . . .

104   105

106   107

104. . . . grips it and . . .

105. . . . pulls it as she starts to turn clockwise.

106. Continuing to turn, she wheels him around and places her left forearm at the back of his elbow, . . .

107. . . . taking him to the mat. She applies light pressure. He taps.

†They rise, ready for the next segment of the kata.

108

109

110

ROUNDHOUSE PUNCH

108. Bruce simulates a roundhouse punch . . .

109, 110. Susan grips his wrist and pulls it as she starts to turn clockwise.

111

112

111, 112. Continuing to turn, she wheels him around and down and applies the hold. He taps.

†They rise, ready for the next segment of the kata.

113

LOW UPPERCUT

113. Bruce simulates a low uppercut.

†Susan parries . . .

114

115

116

117

114. . . . then reaches across his arm and . . .

115. . . . grips his wrist with her right hand and braces her left hand onto her right forearm . . .

116. . . . as she takes a step with her right foot and twists his captured arm back.

117. She takes him to the mat onto his left knee by pulling down on his captured wrist as she braces her left forearm into the bend of his elbow, then . . .

118

119

120

118. . . . starts to drop onto her right knee as she pulls him back . . .

119. . . . onto the mat. He taps.

120. They rise and face each other and bow.

This is the end of the first kata.

SECOND KATA - PETE MILLER & TOM MATCHETT

In the traditional method of teaching aikido, students are
permitted to practice only the routines given to them by the
instructor. It is my experience that students benefit greatly
if they develop original routines in addition to learning forms
devised by others. The creativity which is released through
choreographing new routines allows for self-expression
through movement. Encouraging students to think of
aikido as a living art as well as a traditional, fixed form
is, I believe, a balanced approach.

Using characteristic aikido techniques, Pete Miller and Tom
Matchett first improvised and then performed this original
fourteen-part kata.

Tom does not resist Pete's defense actions and he goes with
Pete's movements. Pete applies very light pressure, allowing
Tom to go to the mat without hurting him; he simulates the
pressure of the ending techniques. By coordinating their
movements, they perform the kata without risk of injury.

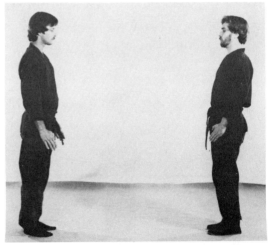

121

121. Tom and Pete start from a position of reflection,
erect but relaxed, their hands at their thighs, their eyes
lowered.

122. They bow to each other.

WRIST GRIP

123. Tom grips Pete's left wrist with his right hand.

124-126. Pete twists his hand out, up and over, to escape from the grip, then . . .

123   124

125

126

127

128

127. . . . Pete grips high under Tom's arm with his right hand and pushes at Tom's forearm with his left hand, and . . .

128. . . . as he steps in with his left foot, Pete grips and bends Tom's captured hand.

129. As he drops to his right knee, Pete takes Tom to the mat and starts to . . .

130

131

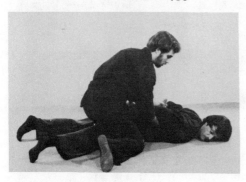

132

130. . . . push Tom's captured bent arm . . .

131. . . . and wheel him around and . . .

132. . . . onto the mat face down. Pete goes with Tom's movement onto the mat to avoid hurting him.

†Tom taps to signal "submission" and they both rise, ready for the next segment.

133

134

135

TWO-HAND GRIP OF ONE WRIST

133. Tom grips Pete's right wrist with both hands.

134. As he steps back counterclockwise with his left foot, Pete grips Tom's left wrist with his left hand and . . .

135. . . . twists his right hand free to grip Tom's right wrist. As he completes his pivot he crosses Tom's arms . . .

136

137

136. . . . pulling Tom's left arm cross-body as he pulls Tom's right arm inward.

137. Tom takes a side rolling fall and Pete goes down on his left knee to assist Tom in taking a safe fall.

†They rise, ready for the next segment.

138

139

140

DOUBLE WRIST GRIP

138. Tom grips Pete's wrists.

139. Pete twists his hands out and . . .

140. . . . over and grips Tom's wrists.

141

142

143

144

141, 142. Maintaining his grips on Tom's wrists, Pete steps and turns clockwise, crossing Tom's arms.

143. Pete drops to his left knee and . . .

144. . . . pulls Tom forward. Tom takes a rolling fall.

†They rise, ready for the next segment.

145

146

147

148

CLOTH GRIP

145. Tom grips cloth high.

146. Pete grips Tom's hand with his left hand and steps with his left foot, . . .

147. . . . turning counterclockwise as he twists Tom's captured hand and pulls it, and places his right hand at the back of Tom's elbow.

148. As Tom goes onto the mat, Pete drops to his right knee and . . .

149. . . . simulates pressing down with his right hand as he bends and twists the captured hand with his left hand.

†They rise, ready for the next segment.

150   151

TWO-HAND CLOTH GRIP

150. Tom grips cloth with both hands.

151. Pete reaches in and over Tom's right wrist with his left hand and . . .

152

153

154

152. . . . braces his right foot against Tom's right foot as he grips Tom's upper arm with his right hand and pulls him . . .

153. . . . around and . . .

154. . . . down onto the mat. He simulates pressure against Tom's captured arm, levering it across his bent left leg.

†They rise, ready for the next segment.

155   156

SHOULDER GRIPS

155. Tom grips Pete's shoulders. Pete puts his hands to-
gether and . . .

156. . . . thrusts upward, then . . .

157. . . . brings his left arm around Tom's right arm,
and . . .

158. . . . draws his left hand into his chest and braces his
right hand at Tom's upper arm. Tom's captured arm is
locked under Pete's arm.

159. Pete presses up with his left arm as he pushes down
with his right hand, levering . . .

160. . . . Tom around and down.

†They rise, ready for the next segment.

157

158

159

160

161

162

163

TWO-HAND REACH

161. Tom reaches with both hands. Pete dodges to his left and . . .

162. . . . parries with his right forearm, then . . .

163. . . . places his left hand at Tom's upper arm as he reaches around with his right hand to . . .

164

165

166

164. . . . clasp Tom's head and . . .

165. . . . twists Tom around and . . .

166. . . . down. As Tom goes down, Pete drops to his left knee and bows Tom across his bent leg.

†They rise, ready for the next segment.

167

168

169

170

OVER-ARMS BODY GRAB FROM THE BACK

167. Tom grabs Pete from behind, around both arms.

168. Pete thrusts his arms up, . . .

169. . . . grips Tom's right wrist with his right hand and . . .

170. . . . grips Tom's left hand with his left hand as he takes a step back (behind his right foot) with his left foot, . . .

171   172

173

171. . . . turning counterclockwise and releasing his left hand grip as he twists Tom's captured hand and . . .

172. . . . raises it as he places his left hand at Tom's upper arm.

173. As he takes Tom to the mat by pressing down with his right hand and pulling inward with his left hand, Pete goes onto his left knee.

†They rise, ready for the next segment.

174

175

176

SHOULDER GRAB FROM THE BACK

174. Tom grips Pete's shoulders.

175. Pete grips both of Tom's wrists and . . .

176. . . . pulls forward, then thrusts his arms up and . . .

177

178

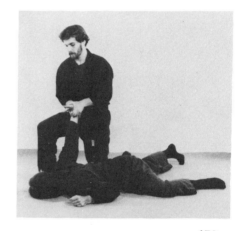
179

177. . . . steps around counterclockwise with his left foot
as he grips Tom's right wrist with his right hand and . . .

178. . . . swings Tom's captured arm in an arc down and then
back. He grips the captured hand with both hands. His
thumbs are braced onto the back of Tom's hands, his
fingers are into the palm.. . .

179. He takes Tom to the mat by bending and twisting the
captured hand and goes onto his left knee.

†They rise, ready for the next segment.

180   181

182

FINGER CHOKE FROM THE BACK

180. Tom simulates a choke.

181. Pete grips Tom's hands and . . .

182. . . . pulls forward.

183

184

185

186

183. Without releasing his grips, Pete steps counterclockwise to Tom's right side . . .

184. . . . then releases his left hand grip as he pulls Tom's hand down, then . . .

185. . . . out and up. He simulates pressure at the back of Tom's upper arm, then . . .

186. . . . goes down onto his left knee as Tom goes onto the mat.

†They rise, ready for the next segment.

187
188

189
190

FOREARM CHOKE

187. Tom simulates a forearm choke.

188, 189. Using a reverse grip, Pete grips Tom's hand and twists it out and up as he steps to Tom's right side.

190. Pete braces his left foot behind Tom and . . .

191

191. . . . is in position to topple Tom back off-balance and . . .

† . . . lever him down to the mat as he goes down onto one knee to ease Tom's fall. They rise, ready for the next segment.

192

193

STRAIGHT PUNCH

192. Tom simulates a straight punch, which Pete parries with his open right hand.

193. He grips Tom's hand and . . .

194, 195. . . . turns clockwise as he pulls Tom's captured hand over his right shoulder and . . .

196. . . . goes onto his left knee.
†Tom takes a rolling fall forward . . .

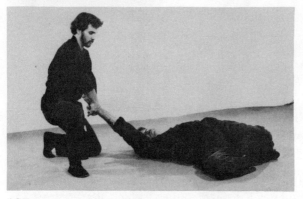

197. . . . and is supine on the mat.
†They rise, ready for the next segment.

198

199

200

201

MID-BODY PUNCH

198. Tom simulates a mid-body punch.

199. Pete parries up under Tom's elbow, then . . .

200. . . . slides his left hand over into the bend of Tom's elbow as he grips and raises Tom's arm. He uses a reverse grip, which allows him to . . .

201. . . . twist and bend the captured hand and arm back as he steps in with his right foot.

202   203

202, 203. He drops onto his left knee as Tom goes down to the mat.

†They rise, ready for the next segment.

204   205

OVERHEAD HAMMER BLOW

204. Tom simulates an overhead hammer blow . . .

205. Pete parries the arm cross-body with his open left hand and . . .

206

207

208

206-208. . . . turns clockwise as he pushes Tom's arm down, back and up. As he turns, he slides his arm under Tom's arm.

209

210

211

209, 210. He pulls the captured arm into his chest and places his right hand at Tom's shoulder. He simulates the pressure which takes Tom to the mat by pulling inward with his left arm as he pushes lightly onto Tom's shoulder.

211. They rise and bow. This is the end of their kata.

KATA SEGMENTS -
DR. AUGUSTO LODI & MR. GEORGE WALLACE

The fifteen kata segments which are demonstrated by
Dr. Lodi and Mr. Wallace have been selected from two
separate routines. They have been chosen to show
characteristics of an older style of aikido than the
preceding katas.

Dr. Lodi, who is an architect and planner, achieved
second degree black belts in judo, karate, and aikido.
Born in Italy, Dr. Lodi took his degrees in Italy and
Venezuela. He became interested in the martial arts
during his residence in Maracaibo, where he studied
aikido with Master Minoru Mochizuki. Mochizuki had
been a student of Master Morihei Uyeshiba, the founder
of aikido. Aikido became Dr. Lodi's favorite pastime.
When he came to Hollywood from Venezuela he con-
ducted an aikido class at my school for several years.

Mr. Wallace was a self-defense instructor at my school
in Hollywood during the 1960's.

The style of aikido which Dr. Lodi learned from Mochizuki
retains features showing its direct derivation from jujitsu
techniques and is undoubtedly closer to the first forms
of aikido called *aiki jitsu*. In addition to a noticeably
different style of gesture, the use of simulated atemi hand
blows suggests the transition from the older style, which
reflected a "hard" jujitsu tradition, to the present "soft"
mode of aikido.

In references found in the earliest books describing aikido,
it is called a "secret" art which could not be made generally
available to the public because one blow of aikido could
kill an opponent.

212

213

214

215

WRIST GRIP

212. Wallace grips Lodi's right wrist. Lodi simulates an
atemi punch into the face with his left hand and . . .

213. . . . grips Wallace's left hand with his left hand as he
releases the captured wrist by thrusting down sharply,
and without hesitation . . .

214. . . . Lodi starts a counterclockwise turn, stepping
toward Wallace with his right foot, and gripping Wallace's
left hand with both hands.

215. Lodi raises the captured hand and continues to turn
and duck under Wallace's arm to complete the turn and
bend the captured hand back, as shown.

216. As Lodi applies the wrist-and-shoulder twisting pressure with his left hand (assisted by his forward body movement) Wallace takes a rolling back fall.

†Lodi releases the captured hand to allow Wallace to complete his fall safely.

WRIST GRIP

217. Wallace grips Lodi's right wrist. Lodi simulates an atemi punch . . .

†. . . and releases his captured wrist by twisting it around and out.

218. With his left hand Lodi grips Wallace's left wrist as he thrusts his right arm under Wallace's captured arm and takes a deep step with his right foot. Lodi simulates a wrist/arm hold by pressing slightly upward with his right upper arm as he presses lightly down on the captured wrist, then . . .

217   218

219

220

221

219. . . . Lodi clamps his right hand over his own left hand and pulls Wallace's captured hand into his chest.

220. As Wallace prepares to take a forward rolling fall, Lodi bends forward and . . .

221. . . . twists his body counterclockwise to assist and follow Wallace's movement.

†Lodi releases his grip as Wallace rolls over.

REVERSE WRIST GRIP

222. Wallace grips Lodi's right wrist using a reverse grip (with the thumb pointing down). Lodi simulates an atemi punch with his left hand.

223. As he thrusts his right hand upward, Lodi starts to grip Wallace's left wrist with his left hand.

222   223

224   225

†Lodi twists his captured wrist free and grips Wallace's left wrist with his right hand and . . .

224. . . . pulls and extends the captured arm around and down, turning it palm up.

225. Lodi thrusts his right arm under the captured arm as he takes a deep step with his right foot.

†Lodi is in position to apply the arm/wrist hold and completes the action by levering Wallace forward, releasing the grip as Wallace takes a rolling fall.

226   227

DOUBLE SLEEVE GRIP

226. Wallace grips both sleeves. Lodi thrusts his open right right hand toward Wallace's face as a distracting feint.

227, 228. Lodi makes a circular movement with his right arm, outward and over Wallace's left arm and as the circular movement is completed, Lodi grips Wallace's left hand with his left hand and . . .

229. . . . takes a deep step with his right foot as he grips Wallace's left hand with his right hand (now both hands are gripping) and he begins a counterclockwise turn.

230. As the turn is completed, Lodi applies a wrist-and-shoulder twist with his left hand.

†As Wallace takes a back rolling fall, Lodi releases his grip.

DOUBLE WRIST GRIP

231. Wallace grips both wrists. Lodi thrusts both arms outward, and without hesitation . . .

232. . . . pulls both arms inward sharply to effect release of his right hand.

†Then he twists his left wrist free and grips Wallace's left wrist with his left hand.

233. As Lodi takes a deep step with his right foot, he pulls and turns the captured hand palm up and thrusts his right arm under Wallace's arms.

†Lodi is in position to simulate the arm/wrist hold and apply the levering action which pulls Wallace forward. As Wallace rolls, Lodi releases his grip.

228   229

230

231

232   233

234

235

236

23

DOUBLE LAPEL GRIP

234. Wallace grips both lapels. Lodi simulates an atemi punch, then . . .

235. . . . he ducks his head down between Wallace's arms and starts to rise to the outside of Wallace's left arm, and . . .

236. . . . thrusts his arms sharply upward and . . .

237. . . . applies a levering action with his right arm onto Wallace's upper left arm.

†Lodi continues the levering action, taking Wallace to the ground, face down.

238   239

GRAB & PUNCH

238. Wallace grips with his right hand and simulates a left uppercut.

239. Lodi starts a counterclockwise turn, stepping around with his right foot as he parries Wallace's left arm with his forearm and starts to grip Wallace's left hand with his left hand.

240   241

240. As he continues to turn, Lodi pulls the captured arm with both his arms . . .

241. . . . and completes the turn to duck under Wallace's arm, raising it in position to apply a wrist-and-shoulder twist.

†As Wallace takes rolling back fall, Lodi releases his grip.

242

243

244

245

FRONT CHOKE

242. Wallace simulates a front choke. Lodi simulates a punch with his right fist, then . . .

243. . . . he grips Wallace's left wrist with both his hands and . . .

244. . . . pulls the captured arm as he begins a counter-clockwise turn, . . .

245. . . . ducking under the captured arm to complete the turn, raising and bending Wallace's arm in position for the wrist-and-shoulder twist.

†Wallace takes a rolling back fall and Lodi releases his grip as Wallace falls.

246   247

248   249

DOUBLE LAPEL GRIP

246. Wallace grips both lapels. Lodi simulates an atemi blow with his right fist.

247. He grips Wallace's left wrist with both his hands and begins a counterclockwise turn, ducking his head down between the arms . . .

248. . . . continuing the turn and . . .

249. . . . raising and bending Wallace's captured arm into position for the wrist-and-shoulder twist.

†As Wallace takes a rolling back fall, Lodi releases his grip.

250

251

252

HAIR PULLING

250. Wallace simulates hair pulling. Lodi simulates an atemi punch with his left fist.

251. As he grips Wallace's left hand with his left hand, he thrusts his right hand up and . . .

252. . . . steps in with his right foot, twisting and lifting the captured hand and applying light pressure onto the back of the elbow with his right forearm.

†Lodi takes Wallace to the mat, face down.

253

254

255

TWO-HAND REACH

253. Wallace reaches with both hands. Lodi blocks the reaching hands with crossed hands and . . .

254. . . . grips Wallace's right wrist with both hands as he steps and turns clockwise with his left foot and pulls the captured arm and twists the wrist.

†Lodi then raises the captured arm and ducks under it as he continues to turn clockwise.

255. At the completion of the turn, Lodi has released his left hand grip and holds Wallace's wrist with his right hand. He bends the captured arm back and down . . .

† . . . to take Wallace to the mat. Wallace takes a rolling back fall and Lodi releases his grip as Wallace goes down.

256   257

258   259

REAR DOUBLE WRIST GRIP

256. Wallace grips both wrists from the back. As Lodi takes a step with his right foot . . .

257. . . . he thrusts his right arm up and thrusts his left arm down, escaping the grips and . . .

† . . . turns counterclockwise . . .

258. . . . facing Wallace. He grips Wallace's left hand with both his hands.

259. He continues to turn counterclockwise, ducking under the captured arm and . . .

260

260. . . . as he completes the turn, he releases his right
hand grip. With his left hand he bends Wallace's arm back
and down.

†As Wallace takes a rolling fall back Lodi releases his grip.

REAR DOUBLE WRIST GRIP

261. Wallace grips both wrists from the back. Lodi thrusts
both arms forward, then . . .

262. . . . pivots and turns counterclockwise as he thrusts
his right arm up and drops his left arm.

261   262

263

263. Lodi continues to turn counterclockwise, capturing Wallace's left wrist and thrusting his right arm under the captured arm. He applies pressure upward with his right arm under Wallace's arm as he pulls down on the captured wrist.

†He wheels Wallace around and forward. Wallace takes a forward rolling fall and Lodi releases his grip as Wallace goes down.

264

265

266

267

DOUBLE SLEEVE GRIP FROM THE BACK

264. Wallace grips both sleeves. Lodi thrusts his arms forward as he takes a step with his right foot . . .

265. . . . then thrusts his right hand up and thrusts his left hand down . . .

266, 267. . . . turning counterclockwise to face Wallace. He grips Wallace's left hand with both his hands and twists and raises the captured hand . . .

† . . . to wheel Wallace down and around onto the mat. He releases his grip as Wallace falls.

268

269

270

271

CHOKE & WRIST GRIP

268. Wallace simulates a choke and grips Lodi's left wrist. Lodi thrusts his left hand outward . . .

269. . . . then upward as he simulates an atemi hand blow back.

270. He turns clockwise to face Wallace and grip Wallace's right hand.

271. He continues to turn as he twists the captured hand and wrist. Wallace goes with Lodi's action and . . .

†Lodi is in position to apply the pressure which takes Wallace forward. Wallace takes a rolling forward fall and Lodi releases him for a safe ending.

BOKATA

Most schools of aikido include bokata (also called jokata) as part of their training.

The katas are series of blocking, parrying, thrusting, and striking moves, simulating defense actions with counterattacks, using a long staff.

Body movement and gestures are graceful, flowing and continuous. The thrusts, blocks and strikes are performed with dynamic, focused energy.

The staff is held with a light enough grasp to allow easy transition from one move to the next. The stylized character of bokata is clearly evident in the moves where the staff is held in the "Y" of the hand, between the thumb and index finger. In this position the staff would be useless for "real" defense or attack. For kata demonstration, this manner of holding the staff adds to the formalized beauty of the movements.

The staff has no recognizable point or butt. To describe the actions, the forward-pointing tip of the staff will be called the point; the rear-facing tip will be called the butt. Either end of the staff can be point or butt.

272   273   274

SOLO STAFF KATA - JOHNNY MIDDLETON

272. Johnny begins the form standing in an erect, relaxed stance, holding the staff in a natural grip with his left hand and using a reverse grip (thumb pointing down) with his right hand.

273. As he takes a step back with his right foot and turns his body to face toward his right side, he raises the stick and slides his left hand toward the tip and blocks upward. The staff is held lightly in the "Y" of his hands.

274. He thrusts, and then . . .

275. . . . raises the staff into a high guard, then . . .

276. . . . parries outward.

277. Without foot movement, Johnny turns to face front as he regrips the middle of the staff with his right hand and starts to regrip the tip, ready to . . .

278. . . . take a step with his right foot as he strikes downward, then . . .

279. . . . draws his left foot back as he blocks low and regrips the butt, palm forward.

275

276

277

278

279

280   281   282

280, 281. As he takes a step forward with his left foot,
Johnny twirls the staff by bringing his left hand forward
and down as he raises his right hand and . . .

282. . . . without hesitation, he continues to turn clockwise,
pivoting on both feet and he . . .

283. . . . takes a step to the rear with his left foot as he
draws the staff to a vertical high block position.

284. He raises his left hand and . . .

285. . . . delivers a low block.

286. He raises his right hand and . . .

287. . . . delivers a high forward strike.

283   284

285   286   287

288

289

290

291

288. He raises his left hand and draws his right hand down and back and . . .

289. . . . up as he prepares to . . .

290. . . . step with his right foot and deliver a high strike.

291. He draws his left hand back and starts to regrip with his right hand, using a reverse grip and . . .

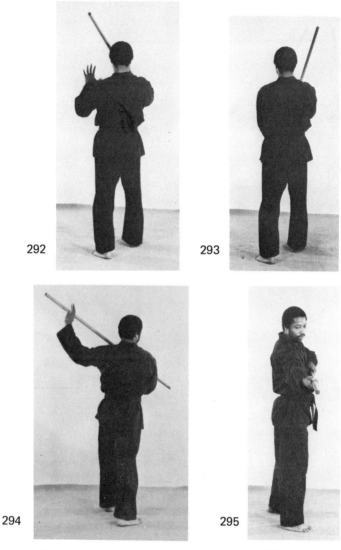

292. . . . delivers a one-handed slashing strike. Without hesitation . . .

293. . . . he grips the butt with his left hand and delivers a second slashing strike.

294. As he steps back with his right foot, and starts to pivot clockwise, he raises his left hand and starts to draw his right hand down . . .

295. . . . to bring the staff into a horizontal position as he completes the pivot and . . . thrusts and . . .

296   297   298

296. . . . takes a step forward with his right foot as he draws the staff back.

297. As he takes a step with his left foot, he draws his right hand back and brings his left hand forward and then . . .

298. . . . down to hold the staff in a vertical position for a high block.

299. As he steps forward with his right foot, Johnny slides his right hand up and starts to bring his left hand back to . . .

300. . . . put the staff in a horizontal position with his right hand forward. He delivers a thrust.

301. He drops back onto his left knee as he draws the staff back. (This is an evasive movement.)

302. As he rises, he raises the staff above his head and . . .

303. . . . as he steps forward with his left foot, he draws his right hand back and . . .

299

300

301

302

303

304   305   306

307   308

304. . . . up as he rotates the staff and blocks upward.

305. He steps back with his left foot as he draws the staff up and back and then . . .

306, 307. . . . delivers a downward thrust as he steps with his left foot.

308. He steps forward with his right foot and ends the kata in the starting position.

SOLO STAFF KATA - TOM MATCHETT

309. Tom begins the kata standing erect and relaxed, with the staff held in front of him, positioned in the "Y" of both hands.

310. As he steps forward with his left foot, he grips the staff and draws it back to his right side, preparing to . . .

311. . . . deliver a thrust forward.

309   310   311

312. Raising his right arm and opening his hands for the "Y" block position, he . . .

312

313   314   315

313. . . . rotates the staff in a high arc, and . . .

314, 315. . . . as he steps forward with his right foot, Tom releases his left hand grip and regrips the staff at the butt end with his right hand advanced and . . .

316. . . . delivers a downward strike.

317. He draws the staff back to his left side and . . .

318. . . . raises his left hand and . . .

319. . . . and blocks to his right side and . . .

320. . . . draws the staff back and down and . . .

321. . . . delivers a downward strike.

316

317

318

319

320

321

322   323

324   325

322. As he steps behind his left foot with his right foot, he draws the staff back with his left hand, sliding the staff along his open right hand, . . .

323. . . . pivoting on his left foot. He blocks outward and continues to pivot clockwise . . .

324. . . . to face to the rear and block to his left side.

325. He draws the staff back and up with his right hand and . . .

326. . . . raises it to a high vertical position for a block.
327,328. He regrips the staff with his right hand in a reverse grip and blocks to his left side.
329. Releasing his left hand grip, he strikes one-handed.

330, 331. He regrips with his left hand and delivers a two-handed strike downward.

332, 333. He draws the staff back and up with his left hand as he turns clockwise to . . .

334

335

336

337

338

334. . . . deliver a thrust to the front.

335. Without foot movement, Tom looks to the rear as he draws the staff back to . . .

336. . . . deliver a thrust to the rear.

337. He steps back and around with his right foot and turns clockwise to . . .

338. . . . face front with his body turned to his right side.

339   340   341

342   343   344

339-342. He blocks upward and draws the staff back to deliver a forward thrust, followed by a high block.

343. He changes the "Y" grip of his left hand to grip the staff palm down and releases his right hand grip to . . .

345

346

347

348

349

344. . . . regrip the staff with his right hand in front of his left hand and . . .

345. . . . delivers a swinging blow . . .

346. . . . downward.

347. He draws the staff back with his right hand and . . .

348. . . . delivers a forward thrust.

349. He steps back with his left foot to assume the starting stance and finishes the kata with the staff held in a vertical position.

SOLO STAFF KATA - PETE MILLER

350. Pete starts the form standing in an erect, relaxed stance holding the staff at his side with his right hand.

351, 352. He grasps the staff in a reverse grip with his left hand and takes a step outward with his left foot as he draws the staff cross-body and . . .

350

351

352

353

354

353. . . . blocks downward and then . . .

354. . . . blocks upward.

355

356

357

358

355. He steps back with his left foot and starts to position the staff for a . . .

356. . . . thrust forward.

357. Without foot movement, he ducks (an evasive movement) and blocks up to the rear.

358, 359. As he steps back with his left foot, he draws the staff back and then delivers a thrust with his left hand forward on the staff, followed by . . .

360. . . . a swinging blow which reverses his hand position so that his right hand is advanced.

361. Without foot movement, he blocks to the side then . . .

362. . . . thrusts downward.

359

360

361

362

363

364

363, 364. He takes a step, crossing his right foot behind his left foot as he draws the staff cross-body to his right and then delivers a thrust to his left side.

365. He steps around counterclockwise with his left foot, preparing to turn 180 degrees and . . .

366. . . . thrusts down and then . . .

367. . . . thrusts up.

368. He draws the staff cross-body and . . .

65

366

367

368

369

370

369. . . . thrusts. Without hesitation . . .

370. . . . he pivots counterclockwise and blocks up.

371. Stepping with his right foot, he completes the pivot and blocks to the rear, then . . .

372. . . . blocks upward and back.

373. Without foot movement, he draws the staff back and thrusts high.

374. Lowering his left hand, he blocks to the rear with the staff in a vertical position, then . . .

371

372

373

374

375

376

377

375. . . . strikes downward with his right hand advanced on the staff.

376. He draws his right hand up and back to block with the staff in a vertical position.

377. He ducks (an evasive movement) and lowers his right hand and . . .

378. . . . and strikes low to his left by swinging the staff counterclockwise.

379. He turns clockwise and drops to his left knee and thrusts to the rear.

380, 381. Holding the staff with his right hand (bracing it under his right arm) he rises with his left hand in a guard position and . . .

378

379

380

381

382   383

382, 383. . . . swings the staff clockwise as he faces front.

384, 385. He regrips the staff with his left hand and strikes to his right, then . . .

386. . . . strikes upward and . . .

387. . . . draws his left hand back to bring the staff into a horizontal position for an . . .

384

385

386

387

388

389

390

388. . . . arcing blow downward.

389. Pete then assumes a stance with the staff held outward with his right hand. His open left hand and the unguarded posture indicate the end of the "fight."

390. He finishes the form with the staff held at his left side.

INDEX

FOR A FREE BROCHURE describing
our complete line of martial arts books - -
karate, judo, self-defense, kung fu, savate,
aikido, and other special titles in this
field, as well as Ellen Kei Hua's three
inspirational books, write to:

THOR PUB. CO.
P. O. BOX 1782
VENTURA CA 93002